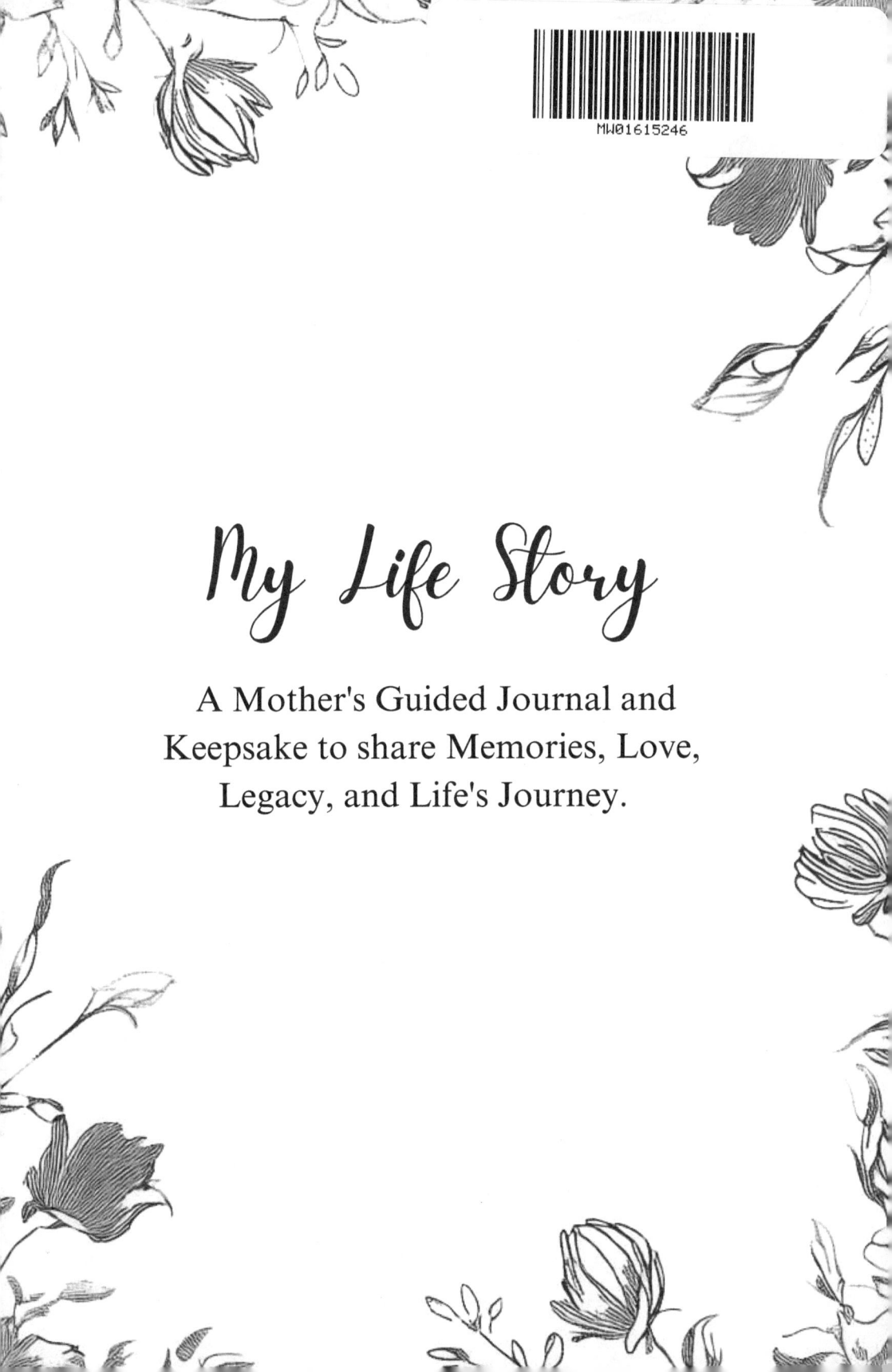

My Life Story

A Mother's Guided Journal and
Keepsake to share Memories, Love,
Legacy, and Life's Journey.

THIS BOOK HOLDS THE MEMOIR OF

_____

Contents

INTRODUCTION

My Life Story - A Mother's Guided Journal and Keepsake to share Memories, Love, Legacy, and Life's Journey.

Every life is a unique journey, filled with moments big and small that shape who we are. This book is your space to reflect on those moments and share the incredible story of your life—the ups and downs, the joys, and the lessons you've gathered along the way.

This is a space to document your experiences, wisdom, and cherished memories, so that future generations can better understand and appreciate the path you've walked.

Why does your story matter? Because it's your legacy. This isn't just a book—it's a bridge between your past and the future. It's one that will inspire your children, grandchildren, and the many others who will come to know you through your words. It's also an opportunity for you to reflect on the rich tapestry of your life—what you've accomplished, the challenges you've faced, the dreams you've realized, and those you've had to let go.

WHAT YOU CAN EXPECT

This book is designed to feel like a conversation. It's a relaxed and informal space for you to reminisce and tell your story in your own words. You'll find prompts throughout that will gently guide you to different parts of your life—from your childhood, schooling, and young adulthood, to marriage, motherhood, and beyond.

You don't need to worry about writing a perfect "memoir" or trying to sound a certain way. Think of it as talking to a dear friend over a cup of tea, sharing memories and thoughts as they come. The questions and prompts are here to inspire you, but don't feel pressured to answer everything all at once or in a certain order. Skip around if you like, or linger on the memories that bring you the most joy.

HOW TO USE THIS BOOK

It's your book, and you can approach it however feels most comfortable for you. There are no rules—just start wherever you feel inspired. This is your life story, after all—filled with emotions, memories, and lessons that reflect the beauty of living.

A GIFT FOR FUTURE GENERATIONS

As you fill out this book, think about the gift you're giving to your family. You're creating something truly precious—a keepsake that will be treasured by your children, grandchildren, and beyond. This book will allow them to step into your shoes, walk through your memories and experiences, and carry a piece of you with them always.

Your story is not just about the facts of what happened, but about who you are. It's about what shaped you, what you've learned, and how you've grown over the years. So, as you flesh out these pages, remember to be proud of your story, and know that it's one worth telling.

Here's to your journey, and to the many stories waiting to be told.

Early Days

Where it all began...

SHARE THE DETAILS OF
YOUR BIRTH

What were your date and
time of birth?

What was your birth weight
and length?

Were you expected on this day?

Where were you born?

What name was given to you
when you were born?

What color were your eyes and
hair when you were born?

Who was the first person
to hold you?

Who was present during
your birth?

Are there any stories from the day you were born?

_____

_____

_____

_____

_____

_____

_____

_____

_____

_____

_____

BABY PHOTO HERE

Family

Family is about the relationships that
provide emotional security, comfort,
and a sense of identity.

What does family mean to you?

_____

_____

_____

_____

_____

_____

Share about your parents and siblings, and where you fit in your family.

_____

_____

_____

_____

_____

_____

_____

_____

_____

_____

_____

_____

_____

_____

_____

_____

Describe your family life.

_____

_____

_____

_____

_____

_____

_____

_____

_____

_____

_____

_____

_____

_____

_____

_____

_____

_____

_____

_____

_____

_____

_____

_____

_____

_____

_____

_____

_____

_____

How did your parents influence the person you became?

_____

_____

_____

_____

_____

_____

_____

_____

_____

_____

What role did siblings or other relatives play in your life?

_____

_____

_____

_____

_____

_____

_____

_____

_____

_____

_____

_____

How did family challenges or conflicts affect you?

_____

_____

_____

_____

_____

_____

_____

_____

_____

_____

_____

_____

What is the most important thing you've learned from your family?

_____

_____

_____

_____

_____

_____

_____

_____

_____

_____

_____

What were some of the challenges you faced growing up?

_____

_____

_____

_____

_____

_____

_____

_____

_____

_____

Was there a person, place, or activity that helped you through tough times?

_____

_____

_____

_____

_____

_____

_____

_____

_____

_____

ADDITIONAL THOUGHTS

Favorite Childhood Memories

Childhood is all about exploration,
curiosity, wonder and expression

What were you like as a child?

What traditions, memories or experiences from childhood do you treasure?

_____

_____

_____

_____

_____

_____

_____

_____

_____

_____

_____

_____

_____

_____

_____

_____

_____

_____

_____

Who was your role model/hero when you were a child? Why?

_____

_____

_____

_____

_____

_____

_____

What was your family home like and did it have any special areas?

Describe what 'family time' meant.

_____

_____

_____

_____

_____

_____

_____

_____

_____

_____

_____

_____

_____

_____

_____

What were your regular chores?

_____

_____

_____

Did you get a regular allowance?

_____

_____

_____

Childhood friends

Childhood friends are special
individuals with whom
we share our first adventures,
secrets, and dreams.

Who are and how did you meet your closest friends as a child?

_____

_____

_____

_____

_____

_____

_____

_____

_____

_____

_____

What did you do for fun with your friends?

_____

_____

_____

_____

_____

_____

_____

_____

_____

_____

_____

Do you have funny or favorite memories with your childhood friends?

_____

_____

_____

_____

_____

_____

_____

_____

_____

_____

Describe any lifelong friendships you formed as a child.

_____

_____

_____

_____

_____

_____

_____

_____

_____

_____

_____

_____

Community and neighbors

Describe your neighborhood, including your favorite hangout spots.

_____

_____

_____

_____

_____

_____

_____

_____

_____

_____

_____

_____

_____

_____

_____

_____

_____

_____

_____

_____

_____

_____

_____

_____

_____

_____

Who were your neighbors, and were any of them memorable or like family to you?

What was the world like during your childhood?

Popular songs:

_____
_____
_____
_____
_____
_____
_____

Popular television shows:

_____
_____
_____
_____
_____
_____
_____

Popular movies/movie stars:

_____
_____
_____
_____
_____
_____
_____

Popular sports teams:

_____
_____
_____
_____
_____
_____
_____

How much did common household items cost?

_____
_____
_____
_____
_____
_____

Popular sports teams:

_____
_____
_____
_____
_____
_____

What were the significant cultural, social, or political events happening around you?

_____

_____

_____

_____

_____

_____

_____

_____

_____

_____

_____

Was there a major historical event or some technological advancement that stands out from your early years?

_____

_____

_____

_____

_____

_____

_____

_____

_____

_____

_____

_____

How was your overall childhood experience?

School Days

School is super important for both learning and building friendships. It provides knowledge, critical thinking and key social skills such as teamwork, communication, and empathy. School is a balance of increasing independence and building self-discipline & resilience.

What was your first school called? How did you travel to/from school each day?

_____

_____

_____

_____

Share about your first school your memories of being there, and the games you played in the schoolyard.

_____

_____

_____

_____

_____

_____

_____

_____

_____

_____

_____

_____

_____

_____

_____

_____

_____

_____

School ups and downs

How did you cope academically?

_____
_____
_____
_____
_____
_____
_____

What subjects did you enjoy or struggle with the most?

_____
_____
_____
_____
_____
_____
_____

Who was your favorite teacher and why?

_____
_____
_____
_____
_____
_____

How did you handle the school challenges?

_____

_____

_____

_____

_____

_____

_____

_____

_____

_____

Who were the school bullies or the "cool kids," and how did they affect you?

_____

_____

_____

_____

_____

_____

_____

_____

_____

_____

_____

What was the most mischievous thing you did at school?

_____

_____

_____

_____

_____

_____

_____

_____

_____

_____

Were there any school events or moments that stand out?

_____

_____

_____

_____

_____

_____

_____

_____

_____

_____

_____

Making friends at school

Describe one of your first school friends. Do you still keep in touch?

_____

_____

_____

_____

_____

_____

_____

_____

_____

_____

_____

Do you have a favorite memory with a school friend?

_____

_____

_____

_____

_____

_____

_____

_____

_____

_____

_____

_____

After-school fun

What was your routine after school?

_____

_____

_____

_____

_____

_____

_____

_____

_____

_____

Describe the extracurricular activities you were involved in.

_____

_____

_____

_____

_____

_____

_____

_____

_____

_____

_____

Did you have any part-time jobs?

_____

_____

_____

_____

_____

_____

_____

_____

_____

_____

_____

What role did these activities play in your life, and how did they shape you?

_____

_____

_____

_____

_____

_____

_____

_____

_____

_____

_____

_____

teenage Years

The teenage years are often a mix of independence, self-discovery, and growing pains.

What was your nickname?

_____

_____

What was it like being a teenager?

_____

_____

_____

_____

_____

_____

_____

_____

_____

_____

_____

_____

_____

_____

_____

_____

_____

_____

What did you enjoy about school in your teenage years?

_____

_____

_____

_____

_____

_____

_____

_____

_____

How did you feel about homework and exams?

_____

_____

_____

_____

_____

_____

_____

_____

_____

_____

What was your relationship like with your parents and siblings during this time?

_____

_____

_____

_____

_____

_____

_____

_____

_____

_____

_____

Was there a constant argument you had with your parents?

_____

_____

_____

_____

_____

_____

_____

_____

_____

_____

_____

_____

How did you handle peer pressure, school demands, and family expectations?

_____

_____

_____

_____

_____

_____

_____

_____

_____

_____

_____

Did you have any teenage adventures or rebellious moments?

_____

_____

_____

_____

_____

_____

_____

_____

_____

_____

_____

_____

Share the music, fashion, and trends you enjoyed as a teenager and how you kept up with them.

_____

_____

_____

_____

_____

_____

_____

_____

_____

_____

_____

_____

What dreams or ambitions did you have as a teenager?

_____

_____

_____

_____

_____

_____

_____

_____

_____

_____

_____

_____

Who influenced you the most as a teenager?

_____

_____

_____

_____

_____

_____

_____

_____

_____

_____

_____

What advice would you give your teenage self?

_____

_____

_____

_____

_____

_____

_____

_____

_____

_____

_____

ADDITIONAL THOUGHTS

Young Adulthood

A time of self-definition, growth, and
establishing a personal path.

Higher education and early career choices

How difficult was it to choose a career path?

_____

_____

_____

_____

_____

_____

_____

_____

Did you pursue higher education, an apprenticeship or a job after school and what were the highs and lows of that experience?

_____

_____

_____

_____

_____

_____

_____

_____

_____

_____

_____

_____

_____

Who did you live with at this time? What was that experience like?

What jobs have you had during your life?

_____

_____

_____

_____

_____

_____

_____

_____

_____

_____

_____

Was there a milestone in your career that really changed you?

_____

_____

_____

_____

_____

_____

_____

_____

_____

_____

_____

_____

_____

First independence

What was it like when you first moved out of your parents' home?

_____

_____

_____

_____

_____

_____

_____

_____

_____

_____

_____

How did your relationships with your family evolve as you became more independent?

_____

_____

_____

_____

_____

_____

_____

_____

_____

_____

_____

_____

_____

_____

✻ What kind of family activities did you participate in during this time?

_____

_____

_____

_____

_____

_____

_____

_____

_____

✻ Was there a moment when you felt like you were officially 'adulting'?

_____

_____

_____

_____

_____

_____

_____

_____

_____

_____

_____

Describe a vivid moment from your 'twenties'.

_____

_____

_____

_____

_____

_____

_____

_____

_____

_____

Describe the most impulsive thing your young self did?

_____

_____

_____

_____

_____

_____

_____

_____

_____

_____

_____

Romantic relationships and first loves

What did you enjoy about dating?

_____
_____
_____
_____
_____
_____
_____
_____
_____
_____
_____

Describe the dating challenges.

_____
_____
_____
_____
_____
_____
_____
_____
_____
_____
_____
_____

Describe your first significant relationship.

_____

_____

_____

_____

_____

_____

_____

_____

_____

_____

_____

How did your view of relationships evolve during this time?

_____

_____

_____

_____

_____

_____

_____

_____

_____

_____

_____

_____

_____

Finding your identity

How did your identity and sense of self evolve during this time?

_____
_____
_____
_____
_____
_____
_____
_____
_____
_____

Did you go through any periods of self-doubt or questioning?

_____
_____
_____
_____
_____
_____
_____
_____
_____
_____
_____

How did you handle moments of uncertainty or insecurity?

_____

_____

_____

_____

_____

_____

_____

_____

_____

_____

Describe a moment when you took a leap of faith.

_____

_____

_____

_____

_____

_____

_____

_____

_____

_____

_____

_____

Describe mentors or role models who helped guide you.

ADDITIONAL THOUGHTS

Marriage, Motherhood, and Family Life

At its core, motherhood is about an enduring bond and the willingness to offer unconditional support and love. It's a journey that encourages patience, flexibility, and resilience, as well as moments of immense joy and pride.

Meeting your life partner

What was your dating journey like?

_____
_____
_____
_____
_____
_____
_____
_____

How did you know you were in love?

_____
_____
_____
_____
_____
_____
_____
_____

What were your hopes or expectations about committing for life?

_____
_____
_____
_____
_____
_____
_____

What was the proposal or commitment like?

_____

_____

_____

_____

_____

_____

_____

_____

_____

Describe your wedding/commitment ceremony.

_____

_____

_____

_____

_____

_____

_____

_____

What was the most meaningful moment from your special day?

_____

_____

_____

_____

_____

_____

_____

How did you and your partner adjust to life as a couple?

_____

_____

_____

_____

_____

_____

_____

_____

_____

_____

_____

What were some of the challenges of combining your lives?

_____

_____

_____

_____

_____

_____

_____

_____

_____

_____

_____

_____

_____

Becoming a mother

At its core, motherhood is about an enduring bond and the willingness to offer unconditional support and love. It's a journey that encourages patience, flexibility, and resilience, as well as moments of immense joy and pride.

Describe your initial thoughts about impending motherhood?

_____

_____

_____

_____

_____

_____

_____

_____

_____

_____

Describe your pregnancy experience.

_____

_____

_____

_____

_____

_____

_____

_____

_____

_____

_____

_____

What was your experience of labor and delivery like?

_____

_____

_____

_____

_____

_____

_____

_____

_____

_____

_____

How did you feel the first time you held your first child?

_____

_____

_____

_____

_____

_____

_____

_____

_____

_____

_____

_____

Who were the key people in your support system, at this time?

_____

_____

_____

_____

_____

_____

_____

_____

_____

_____

Expectation vs. Reality - how did your world change and how did you adapt?

_____

_____

_____

_____

_____

_____

_____

_____

_____

_____

_____

_____

the early years of parenthood

How did you handle sleepless nights and the demands of caring for a newborn?

_____

_____

_____

_____

_____

_____

_____

_____

_____

_____

_____

Describe your children's personalities.

_____

_____

_____

_____

_____

_____

_____

_____

_____

_____

_____

_____

What were some of the most memorable 'firsts'?

What were some of the challenges during those early years?

_____

_____

_____

_____

_____

_____

_____

_____

_____

_____

_____

Describe a moment when you felt completely overwhelmed as a mother?

_____

_____

_____

_____

_____

_____

_____

_____

_____

_____

_____

_____

What were some of the small, everyday moments that brought you the most joy in motherhood?

_____

_____

_____

_____

_____

_____

_____

_____

_____

_____

How did you find moments for yourself amid the demands of motherhood?

_____

_____

_____

_____

_____

_____

_____

_____

_____

_____

_____

What role did humor play in your motherhood experience?

_____
_____
_____
_____
_____
_____
_____
_____
_____
_____
_____

What advice would you give to a first time mother?

_____
_____
_____
_____
_____
_____
_____
_____
_____
_____
_____
_____
_____

ADDITIONAL THOUGHTS

Family life and parenting journey

Parenthood is ultimately about unconditional love and commitment. It's a journey that requires selflessness. It's a unique, transformative experience that forever changes one's perspective, priorities, and sense of purpose.

What was your parenting style?

_____

_____

_____

_____

_____

_____

_____

_____

_____

_____

_____

As a mother, what phases of parenting were the hardest for you, and how did you manage them?

_____

_____

_____

_____

_____

_____

_____

_____

_____

_____

_____

_____

_____

What were the most cherished moments of motherhood, and what made them so rewarding?

Did you create family traditions or uphold any special rituals passed down through generations?

Did your views on parenting change as your children grew older?

Balancing family life and other roles

How did you balance your career and motherhood?

_____
_____
_____
_____
_____
_____
_____
_____
_____
_____
_____
_____

How did you balance the demands of parenting with your own personal needs and fulfilment?

_____
_____
_____
_____
_____
_____
_____
_____
_____
_____
_____
_____
_____

What strategies did you develop to manage family routines and responsibilities?

_____

_____

_____

_____

_____

_____

_____

_____

_____

_____

What boundaries did you set to keep balance in family life?

_____

_____

_____

_____

_____

_____

_____

_____

_____

_____

_____

_____

What role did your partner or support network play in balancing family responsibilities?

_____

_____

_____

_____

_____

_____

_____

_____

_____

_____

_____

_____

_____

_____

_____

_____

_____

_____

_____

_____

_____

_____

_____

_____

_____

_____

Did you have any hobbies or interests that helped you recharge?

_____

_____

_____

_____

_____

_____

_____

_____

_____

_____

How did you balance your marriage/relationship and parenthood?

_____

_____

_____

_____

_____

_____

_____

_____

_____

_____

_____

ADDITIONAL THOUGHTS

Faith, Spirituality and Philosophy

Early influences

How did your family influence your views on faith, spirituality and philosophy?

_____
_____
_____
_____
_____
_____
_____
_____
_____
_____

Were there any specific traditions or practices that were important in your household?

_____
_____
_____
_____
_____
_____
_____
_____
_____
_____
_____
_____

Personal beliefs

How have your personal beliefs about faith, spirituality and philosophy evolved over the years?

_____

_____

_____

_____

_____

_____

_____

_____

_____

_____

Were there any significant events or experiences that shaped your views?

_____

_____

_____

_____

_____

_____

_____

_____

_____

_____

_____

_____

Community and Worship

Did you belong to any faith, spiritual or philosophy communities?

_____
_____
_____
_____
_____
_____
_____
_____
_____
_____

How did participating in these communities impact your life?

_____
_____
_____
_____
_____
_____
_____
_____
_____
_____
_____
_____

Practices

What practices or rituals have been meaningful to you?

_____

_____

_____

_____

_____

_____

_____

_____

_____

_____

How have they helped you in your personal growth and well-being?

_____

_____

_____

_____

_____

_____

_____

_____

_____

_____

_____

_____

_____

Challenges and Doubts

Have you ever faced challenges or doubts regarding your beliefs about faith, spirituality and philosophy?

_____
_____
_____
_____
_____
_____
_____
_____
_____
_____

How did you navigate through those times?

_____
_____
_____
_____
_____
_____
_____
_____
_____
_____
_____

Interfaith Experiences

Have you had any experiences with different faiths or spiritual practices?

_____

_____

_____

_____

_____

_____

_____

_____

_____

_____

How did these experiences influence your understanding and appreciation?

_____

_____

_____

_____

_____

_____

_____

_____

_____

_____

_____

_____

Legacy and Teachings

What faith, spirituality and philosophy teachings do you hope to pass on to future generations?

_____

_____

_____

_____

_____

_____

_____

_____

_____

Why are these teachings important to you?

_____

_____

_____

_____

_____

_____

_____

_____

_____

_____

_____

the Later Years

The later years are a period of reflection, fulfillment, and adaptation. It is a time that often brings greater wisdom, perspective, and a renewed focus on what truly matters.

New chapters in life

What was your experience transitioning out of full-time work?

_____
_____
_____
_____
_____
_____
_____
_____
_____

Was it something you looked forward to?

_____
_____
_____
_____
_____
_____
_____
_____
_____
_____

How do you stay interested in life?

_____

_____

_____

_____

_____

_____

_____

_____

_____

_____

How did your role in your family change as your children grew older?

_____

_____

_____

_____

_____

_____

_____

_____

_____

_____

_____

If you became a grandparent, how did that compare to being a parent?

_____

_____

_____

_____

_____

_____

_____

_____

_____

_____

How do you feel seeing your children as parents themselves?

_____

_____

_____

_____

_____

_____

_____

_____

_____

_____

How has your perspective on life changed?

_____

_____

_____

_____

_____

_____

_____

_____

_____

_____

_____

_____

What is your approach to maintaining social connections?

_____

_____

_____

_____

_____

_____

_____

_____

_____

_____

_____

_____

How do you stay active and engaged?

_____

_____

_____

_____

_____

_____

_____

_____

_____

_____

_____

What role does community play for you in your later years?

_____

_____

_____

_____

_____

_____

_____

_____

_____

_____

_____

_____

_____

How have your spiritual beliefs or practices evolved over the years?

_____

_____

_____

_____

_____

_____

_____

_____

_____

_____

How do you handle loss and change as you age?

_____

_____

_____

_____

_____

_____

_____

_____

_____

_____

_____

What do you appreciate most about your daily life now?

_____

_____

_____

_____

_____

_____

_____

_____

_____

_____

_____

_____

_____

_____

_____

_____

_____

_____

_____

_____

_____

_____

_____

_____

_____

ADDITIONAL THOUGHTS

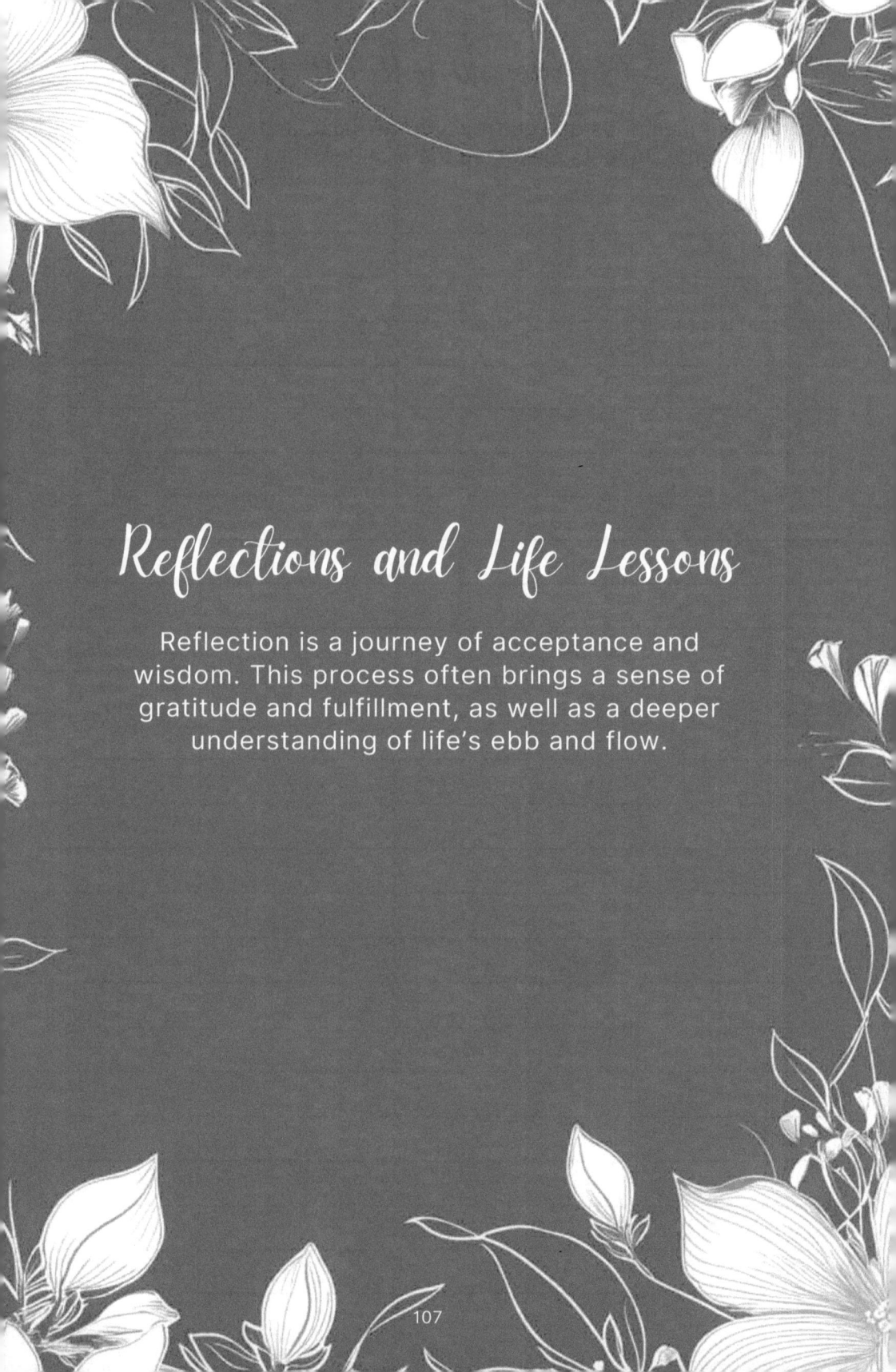

Reflections and Life Lessons

Reflection is a journey of acceptance and wisdom. This process often brings a sense of gratitude and fulfillment, as well as a deeper understanding of life's ebb and flow.

Looking back on life

What memories do you treasure the most, and what accomplishments make you the proudest?

_____

_____

_____

_____

_____

_____

_____

_____

_____

_____

_____

_____

_____

_____

_____

_____

_____

_____

_____

_____

_____

_____

_____

What were the biggest life challenges you faced, and how did they help shape your character?

What are the most significant turning points in your life?

_____

_____

_____

_____

_____

_____

_____

_____

_____

_____

What regrets, if any, do you hold, and what have they taught you?

_____

_____

_____

_____

_____

_____

_____

_____

_____

_____

_____

_____

If you could relive one day of your life, which would it be and why?

_____

_____

_____

_____

_____

_____

_____

_____

_____

_____

_____

What role has love played in your life?

_____

_____

_____

_____

_____

_____

_____

_____

_____

_____

_____

ADDITIONAL THOUGHTS

Lessons learned along the way

What moments taught you the greatest lessons in life, and are there any you wish you'd understood sooner?

_____
_____
_____
_____
_____
_____
_____
_____
_____
_____
_____
_____
_____
_____
_____
_____
_____
_____
_____
_____
_____
_____
_____
_____
_____

What experiences helped you gain perspective on what really matters?

_____

_____

_____

_____

_____

_____

_____

_____

_____

_____

_____

Describe a particular turning point and how it made you rethink your life.

_____

_____

_____

_____

_____

_____

_____

_____

_____

_____

_____

_____

_____

Were there any failures or disappointments that later turned out to be blessings?

_____

_____

_____

_____

_____

_____

_____

_____

_____

_____

Did anyone teach you a life-changing lesson?

_____

_____

_____

_____

_____

_____

_____

_____

_____

_____

_____

_____

Values and beliefs

What core values have guided you through life?

_____

_____

_____

_____

_____

_____

_____

_____

_____

_____

Were there any defining moments that tested or reaffirmed your values?

_____

_____

_____

_____

_____

_____

_____

_____

_____

_____

_____

Have your values and priorities shifted over time?

_____

_____

_____

_____

_____

_____

_____

_____

_____

_____

_____

What role did creativity, spirituality, or introspection play in your values and beliefs?

_____

_____

_____

_____

_____

_____

_____

_____

_____

_____

_____

_____

Looking at the world today

How has the world changed since you were younger?

_____

_____

_____

_____

_____

_____

_____

_____

_____

_____

_____

What is your perspective on modern technology?

_____

_____

_____

_____

_____

_____

_____

_____

_____

_____

_____

_____

What do you think the world could learn from your generation?

Describe your hopes and concerns for the future.

Reflecting on the journey of personal growth

What personal strengths have helped you throughout your life?

_____
_____
_____
_____
_____
_____
_____
_____
_____

What habits, routines, or practices have you adopted to support your personal growth?

_____
_____
_____
_____
_____
_____
_____
_____
_____
_____

What failures or setbacks became an opportunity for personal growth?

_____

_____

_____

_____

_____

_____

_____

_____

_____

_____

_____

Are there learnings from your own character or abilities that you didn't expect?

_____

_____

_____

_____

_____

_____

_____

_____

_____

_____

_____

In what ways do you feel you've changed the most over the years?

_____

_____

_____

_____

_____

_____

_____

_____

_____

_____

_____

_____

_____

_____

_____

_____

_____

_____

_____

_____

_____

_____

_____

_____

_____

_____

_____

the people who've made a difference

Describe someone who was a big influence on your life?

_____
_____
_____
_____
_____
_____
_____
_____
_____
_____
_____

What relationships have been most important to you?

_____
_____
_____
_____
_____
_____
_____
_____
_____
_____
_____
_____
_____

What lessons have you learned from others?

_____

_____

_____

_____

_____

_____

_____

_____

_____

_____

_____

How important have family been to you?

_____

_____

_____

_____

_____

_____

_____

_____

_____

_____

_____

_____

How do you define success now, and how has that changed?

_____

_____

_____

_____

_____

_____

_____

_____

_____

_____

_____

What advice would you give to your younger self?

_____

_____

_____

_____

_____

_____

_____

_____

_____

_____

_____

_____

Legacy and what you'll leave behind

What are you most grateful for in your life?

_____

_____

_____

_____

_____

_____

_____

_____

_____

_____

_____

How do you want to be remembered?

_____

_____

_____

_____

_____

_____

_____

_____

_____

_____

_____

What legacy do you hope to leave for future generations?

ADDITIONAL THOUGHTS

Passing on Some Wisdom

Passing on wisdom is a gift that reflects a desire to empower others, to see them grow and thrive with greater ease.

On life advice

What is the best advice you've ever received?

_____
_____
_____
_____
_____
_____
_____
_____
_____
_____

What have you learned about maintaining meaningful relationships?

_____
_____
_____
_____
_____
_____
_____
_____
_____
_____
_____

✿ What advice would you give to a new parent?

_____

_____

_____

_____

_____

_____

_____

_____

_____

_____

✿ What advice would you give to the parent of a teenager?

_____

_____

_____

_____

_____

_____

_____

_____

_____

_____

_____

_____

On personal growth and change

What experiences in your life sparked the most significant personal growth?

_____

_____

_____

_____

_____

_____

_____

_____

_____

In your opinion, what is the most important action for personal growth?

_____

_____

_____

_____

_____

_____

_____

_____

_____

_____

_____

What's your advice for balancing work, family, and personal passions?

_____

_____

_____

_____

_____

_____

_____

_____

_____

What do you think is the key to staying curious and open to change?

_____

_____

_____

_____

_____

_____

_____

_____

_____

_____

_____

How do you stay positive and hopeful during challenging times?

_____

_____

_____

_____

_____

_____

_____

_____

_____

_____

What's your view on making mistakes and learning from them?

_____

_____

_____

_____

_____

_____

_____

_____

_____

_____

_____

On happiness and contentment

How do you maintain happiness and contentment in difficult times?

_____

_____

_____

_____

_____

_____

_____

_____

_____

What would you say are the keys to long-term happiness?

_____

_____

_____

_____

_____

_____

_____

_____

_____

_____

_____

_____

What role do gratitude and appreciation play in your happiness?

_____

_____

_____

_____

_____

_____

_____

_____

_____

Has mindfulness or living in the moment influenced your happiness?

_____

_____

_____

_____

_____

_____

_____

_____

_____

_____

_____

On future generations

How should people today approach a rapidly changing world?

_____

_____

_____

_____

_____

_____

_____

_____

_____

_____

What do you hope future generations will prioritize?

_____

_____

_____

_____

_____

_____

_____

_____

_____

_____

_____

_____

What advice would you give to future generations?

ADDITIONAL THOUGHTS

Fun Facts

YOU

Introvert or extrovert.

_____

Morning person or night owl?

_____

Boldest thing you have ever done?

_____
_____
_____
_____
_____

Most embarrassed moment?

_____
_____
_____
_____
_____

Best advice you have
ever received?

_____
_____
_____
_____
_____

Worst advice you have
ever received?

_____
_____
_____
_____
_____

What is the best mistake
you ever made?

_____
_____
_____
_____
_____

What is the worst mistake
you ever made?

_____
_____
_____
_____
_____

FOODS AND DRINKS

Favorite food?

Least favored food?

_____

_____

Go-to food for indulgence
or comfort?

Special family recipes?

_____

_____

Favorite drink?

The best junk food ever created?

_____

_____

Craziest thing you've ever eaten?

Who is your ultimate dinner guest?

_____

_____

BOOKS, MOVIES, AND MUSIC

All-time favorite book?

Favorite book from childhood?

_____

_____

Favorite song from childhood?

Favorite movie?

_____

_____

Favorite music genre?

Favorite TV show?

_____

_____

Favorite live performance
experience?

Favorite group/band?

_____

_____

TRAVEL AND ADVENTURE

Pack heavy or light?

_____

City bustle or country quiet?

_____

Relaxing or active adventure?

_____

Favorite travel destination?

_____

Favorite indoor location?

_____
_____

Favorite outdoor location?

_____
_____

Your special place to escape to?

_____
_____
_____
_____

An unforgettable adventure?

_____
_____
_____
_____

An amazing experience that pushed you out of your comfort zone?

_____
_____
_____
_____
_____

A cherished holiday moment?

_____
_____
_____
_____
_____

ACTIVITIES

Favorite relax or unwind activity?

Favorite sports or outdoor activity?

_____

_____

_____

_____

Favorite hobby or pastime?

A hobby you never had time for?

_____

_____

_____

_____

TRADITIONS AND CELEBRATIONS

Favorite special celebration? _____

_____

Favorite family tradition? _____

_____

Favorite way to celebrate achievements? _____

_____

QUIRKS

A surprising fun fact about you?_____

_____

Your unexpected talent? _____

_____

Your most unusual job? _____

_____

Your quirky habit? _____

_____

A routine that you swear by _____

_____

A favorite quote, saying, or mantra that you live by?_____

_____

What do you collect? _____

_____

The most ridiculous fashion you have tried_____

_____

What is on your frivolous spending list? _____

_____

Describe your style in one word_____

Conclusion

As you conclude writing your life story, we hope it's been an enjoyable experience for you. Every chapter represents a unique season of your life—filled with love, challenges, lessons learned, and cherished moments. This book you've written captures the significant milestones and the simple joys that make life meaningful.

Reflecting on a life well-lived allows you to share your memories and experiences, leaving behind a piece of your heart for future generations. More than just a collection of events, it celebrates the moments that shaped the person behind the words.

THE POWER OF SHARING YOUR STORY

Writing and sharing your life story has been a courageous act. It has required introspection, honesty about both triumphs and challenges, and the willingness to share what you've learned with others. This process of looking back has created a piece of wisdom literature that can inspire future generations.

Your story matters. Every life—ordinary or extraordinary—holds value. The experiences detailed in this book offer insights into your choices, love, and lessons learned. By sharing your journey, you've ensured that your memories will endure.

This narrative will establish a lasting connection between the past, present, and future. Future generations will better understand their roots and heritage.

A LASTING LEGACY

Your story creates a legacy that will outlast your time. These words and reflections will serve as guideposts for your family and others who read it. Your narrative isn't just about the past; it may help to shape the future.

CLOSING THOUGHTS

This book encapsulates the essence of your life—the highs, the lows, and everything in between. It is a story that will remind readers of the love, wisdom, and courage that defined your journey. As the final page turns, know that your story has already made an impact. It will continue to touch hearts, inspire minds, and strengthen family bonds for years to come.

Appendices

PARENTS

MOTHER	FATHER
Mother's full name	Father's full name
Mother's date of birth	Father's date of birth
Birthplace	Birthplace
Siblings	Siblings
Location growing up	Location growing up
Schools attended	Schools attended
Employment	Employment

How did your parents meet? _____

_____

_____

_____

_____

_____

Date they got married/committed to each other? _____

_____

What interesting stories have you been told about your parents?

_____

_____

_____

_____

_____

_____

_____

_____

_____

_____

_____

_____

_____

_____

_____

_____

_____

What were some of the most important things you learnt from your mother?

_____

_____

_____

_____

_____

_____

_____

_____

_____

_____

_____

_____

What were some of the most important things you learnt from your father?

_____

_____

_____

_____

_____

_____

_____

_____

_____

_____

_____

_____

GRANDPARENTS

GRANDMOTHER

Maternal grandmother's full name

_____

Maternal grandmother's date
of birth

_____

Birthplace

_____

Siblings

_____

_____

_____

Location growing up

_____

_____

Schools attended

_____

_____

_____

Employment

_____

_____

_____

GRANDFATHER

Maternal grandfather's full name

_____

Maternal grandfather's date
of birth

_____

Birthplace

_____

Siblings

_____

_____

_____

Location growing up

_____

_____

Schools attended

_____

_____

_____

Employment

_____

_____

_____

How did your maternal grandparents meet? _____

_____

_____

_____

_____

_____

Date they got married/committed to each other? _____

_____

What interesting stories have you been told about your maternal
grandparents?

_____

_____

_____

_____

_____

_____

_____

_____

_____

_____

_____

_____

_____

_____

_____

_____

_____

What were some of the most important things you learnt from your maternal grand mother?

_____

_____

_____

_____

_____

_____

_____

_____

_____

_____

_____

What were some of the most important things you learnt from your maternal grandfather?

_____

_____

_____

_____

_____

_____

_____

_____

_____

_____

_____

_____

GRANDPARENTS

GRANDMOTHER

Paternal grandmother's full name

_____

Paternal grandmother's date
of birth

_____

Birthplace

_____

Siblings

_____

_____

_____

Location growing up

_____

_____

Schools attended

_____

_____

_____

Employment

_____

_____

_____

GRANDFATHER

Paternal grandfather's full name

_____

Paternal grandfather's date
of birth

_____

Birthplace

_____

Siblings

_____

_____

_____

Location growing up

_____

_____

Schools attended

_____

_____

_____

Employment

_____

_____

_____

How did your paternal grandparents meet? _____

_____

_____

_____

_____

Date they got married/committed to each other?_____

_____

What interesting stories have you been told about your paternal grandparents?

_____

_____

_____

_____

_____

_____

_____

_____

_____

_____

_____

_____

_____

_____

_____

_____

What were some of the most important things you learnt from your paternal grandmother?

_____

_____

_____

_____

_____

_____

_____

_____

_____

_____

What were some of the most important things you learnt from your paternal grandfather?

_____

_____

_____

_____

_____

_____

_____

_____

_____

_____

_____

My Family Tree

Your Legacy

Thank you so much for purchasing My Life Story - A Mother's Guided Journal and Keepsake to share Memories, Love, Legacy, and Life's Journey. And thankyou for embarking on this journey of self-reflection and storytelling.

I'm truly honored that you've chosen to share your story through the pages of this book. The time and care you've taken to fill in these memories and reflections are a beautiful gift—not only to yourself but to your family and future generations. I know it's not always easy to look back on a lifetime of experiences, emotions, and growth, and I appreciate that you've taken this brave step.

Through your words, you're creating a precious keepsake that will allow your loved ones to see the world through your eyes, learn from your experiences, and feel connected to the legacy you've built. I hope this process has brought you moments of joy, comfort, and self-discovery, as well as the satisfaction of knowing your journey will live on through those who read it.

Thank you again for entrusting My Life Story with your memories and for putting in the time and heart to make this keepsake so meaningful.

Your story matters, and it is a true privilege to be part of helping you tell it.

Beccie A Smith
Author

My Life Story
A Mother's Guided Journal and Keepsake to share
Memories, Love, Legacy, and Life's Journey

Made in United States
Troutdale, OR
03/22/2025

29956372R00096